GENTLEMEN'S RELISH

Poets, like mothers, care less for the praise bestowed on the one child than for the neglect of the rest of the family which they think to be implied.

—Saintsbury, *The Peace of the Augustans*

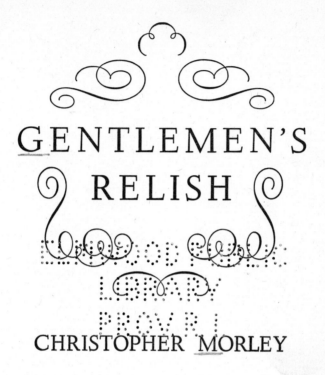

GENTLEMEN'S RELISH

CHRISTOPHER MORLEY

W · W · NORTON & COMPANY · INC · New York

The poems entitled *Shakespeare in Junior High*, *Wasting Shakespeare's Time*, *The Apes*, *150th Anniversary of the Edinburgh Review*, *The Sub-Image*, *Avant-Garde*, *Birth of a Journalist*, *Didn't Call*, *Instrument Disconnected*, *Autobiography*, and *Deny Everything* were first printed as a group in *The Spectator*, November 21, 1952, as *Old Mandarin's Christmas Tree with Twelve Candles*, and are reprinted by permission of *The Spectator*.

The poem entitled *Britain for the Holidays* was first printed in *The Saturday Book*, volume XII, 1952, and is reprinted by permission.

PRINTED IN THE UNITED STATES OF AMERICA
FOR THE PUBLISHERS BY THE VAIL-BALLOU PRESS

In happiest memory of
FRANCIS BARTON GUMMERE (1855–1919)
'myn owene maister deere'
born one hundred years ago
and still, for his pupils, truly alive.

ACKNOWLEDGMENT

Most of these poems were written since April 23, 1951. You will forgive my remembering the exact date, when a sudden and quite unforeseen illness caused a severe change in the writer's life. This has involved a good deal of apparent indolence and dolce far niente. Imagine an old experienced commuter who admits that the last time he climbed aboard a Long Island train was in April, 1951.

I should mention with gratitude those who first printed some of these verses: *The Saturday Review* (N.Y.), *Good Housekeeping, The Atlantic, Harper's, The New York Times Book Review, The New York Herald Tribune, The American Mercury, The Freeman, The Spectator* (London), *The Saturday Book,* vol. 12 (London, 1952). Quite a few have never been in print before.

Two exceptions however. I include by kind permission two poems (I do not tell you which they are) that have appeared in a previous book. No reader, whether professional or amateur, ever seemed to notice or mention them. But I venture to reprint because they are (in my secret fidelities) so plainly moved by generic passions implanted by a beloved teacher nearly half a century ago. I think he would have been pleased by them. That is a teacher's immortality. So I give them here their second chance.

I often wish I might publish enough books to use (as mottoes) my favorite quotes from noble old Saintsbury. In one of his essays he said "persistent self-delusion about literary powers is, except in the case of poets, exceedingly rare."

Even the mention of Professor Saintsbury, with all his curious crotchets, is an echo of Professor Gummere. F.B.G. used to advise us to read him. Of course we never did until years afterward. Understanding often comes too little and too late.

Roslyn Heights, Long Island   C.M.
August 24, 1954

CONTENTS

GENTLEMEN'S RELISH

The Tutor

I was wondering how to spin
A lyric for my youngest kin
 (Exactly three days old)
When in the garden's twilight hush
I was accosted by a thrush
 Unusually bold.

Diving from the dogwood tree,
Not four yards off he studied me;
 His speckle-vest erected,
Then, with beak so open-wide
That I could see his pink inside,
 His lesson he projected.

Three-toned, the treble-warbled note
Came all native from his throat,
 Incomparable flautist!
He gazed, tutorial, to say
That, glissando, is the way,
 In case you never noticed.

All of a sudden he took shy,
Embarrassed-like; and so did I.
 A firefly lit a taper—
Thrush pretended to take a bath,
While I went in across the path
 And found this piece of paper.

and

Elected Silence: Three Sonnets

(In Loving Memory of William Rose Benét, 1886–1950)

I

This was my song, unsingable, unsung;
Long put aside in grieving or in sloth:
Such heaviness to raise the simple word
(How well we knew, is likeliest unheard)
The brain, the good gray dishclout, to be wrung.
Brain split? Fatigue, or indolence, or both?
But mute in midnight now, forgotten man
(No phone will ring) his memory might plan.
Yet (as you said) I was at whiles too clever
In selfish craft and curious fashioning:
Oh why, why did I ever
Do anything but sing?

II

Our time was late for singing, blessed Bill!
We sang: we reeled our purple *qwertyuiop*
As our gaffers would have pared a quill,
Took *fin-de-siècle* by the forward top.
Did sidekick duty in our Grub-street shop
And ribbed each other plenty. You might say
Something of mine was corn and sugar-pop—
I cracked, *You* should know, William Prose Benét.
We laughed, and loved us more. Too late for song?
Sure, singing hath no age? Tremble lives long.
I spoke you always as my Wilhelm Meister,
Shy, and shyer yet, but never shyster.
What 1900 japes and *bouts rimés*
We had: but we were singing all the way.

III

So . . . so . . . each poet has his secret faith
That somewhere, somewhen, someone might arise,
Might read him with unfashionable eyes,
Critic uncrazed by momentary scathe,
So skilled in loves or laughters and/or lust
Dissects the formal flaky pastrycrust
To our god-orchard deepdish fruit below. . . .
And now no postage-stamp will let you know.
We saw men in their universal blitz
Tear our bicycle-boyhood world to bits,
Yet also saw tree, ocean surf, and hill
In the morn's morning measured fresh and new.
My faith, such as it is (not much), dear Bill
Is partly faith in you.

Dusk in the North Wing of a College Library

Swift as the twilight bird
    Tunnels in privet blossom,
Straight as the homesick word
    Into the middle bosom,

These, unerring, steered
    Weaving the sweethour's music;
Words and wings endeared
    Became the English Basic.

Trill the lawnmower snores,
    Lazy the sunlight westers
Slow as cricketing scores
    In Hampshires or in Leicesters—

But all I only crave
    When greens are shadow-slanted
Is talk beyond the grave,
    Unearthly and enchanted.

I have abandoned me,
    But here, in printed musk
Unblemished prosody
    Divisioned in the dusk.

Atomic Fission, April 1387

Whan that Aprille, douce and pluviale . . .

Hand halted. Ink was pending in the fork
Where two tongues divided, equal twins.
Down the hairline of the slitten quill
Language in poise.

                        He looked outdoors
On Kentish spring—fresh as a *marguerite?*
Fresh as a *day's eye* we say in Our Town?

The barnyard pinion dipped deep in the horn,
Struck, and rewrote:
Whan that Aprille with his shoures soote. . . .

English was born.

Public Beach
(Long Island Sound)

The swart Italian with his breast of fur
Soothes bambina when her toe she stubs;
The Baltic blonde (Oh slim! my love to her!)
Adjusts the jerkin that creeps up her chubs,
But all her thought and gaze are offshore where
Two flaxhead boys swash rubber tubes adrift.
Grandpa with his babe plays Old Gray Mare:
"He learns to valk on stones. Now we make lift."

A surf of children tumbles on the sand:
Teuton, Spaniard, Negro, Chinese, Balt,
From all distemper and apartheid free.
Replete with franks and mustard, I understand:
Nakedly primed with universal salt,
Lo, a new people rises from the sea.

Ballad of New York, New York

Around the bend of Harbor Hill
   Comes Number 33,
Says: Board the cars, my bonny boy,
   And ride to Town with me.

A Town that has no ceiling price,
   A Town of double-talk;
A Town so big men name her twice,
   Like so: N'Yawk, N'Yawk.

Then spake the old Belittlin' Witch:
   "Beware the crowded trains;
Of all towns she's the Biggest Bitch—
   Bide here, and save your brains.

"What though she numbers boroughs five
   With many a noble spot,
Her thought is mostly gin and jive,
   Her repartee, So What?"

Himself replied: "Old Gloomy Spook,
   I fear no blatherskites,
I'll blow my nickel in the juke
   Behind the neon lights.

"Or I might even show 'em
   At Sardi's or The Stork—
I feel to write a poem
   About New York, New York."

THE WITCH:—

She's Run-around, and In-and-Out,
   And futile To-and-Fro,

19

And then what it was All About
    You will not even know.

She'll ring you mad by telephone
    And foul your wits with ink;
Men's tricks to get their product shown
    I will not say. They stink.

Across the fifty nations
    Her yokel accents go,
Her mispronunciations
    Broadcast by radio.

When ever did New York requite
    The glamor poets lent her?
Her soul is café-socialite,
    A simian garment-center.

HIMSELF:—

The Town is what you make it
    Of glory and of pain;
I've earned the right to take it
    As Comédie Humaine.

For I have watched her faces
    To educate my soul,
Been drunk in public places
    With bliss, not alcohol.

Yes, I have known a crosstown street
    In sunset parallel
Where lovers lay in peace so sweet
    They never heard the El.

And I have stood, alone, alone,
  Where ships blew hoarse for sea
And armored planes were crowded on
  Like blackbirds on a tree.

The worm is on her portal?
  The Dollar is her joss?
Her sin is, being mortal?
  I enter: *Nolle Pros.*

THE WITCH:—

Okay. Then learn the answers,
  Eternally crack wise,
And be among the dancers
  With belladonna eyes.

Okay. All doors cry Welcome
  (If only Name you bring)
To swamis who talk talcum
  Or poets who can't sing.

Okay. Her mind still plays with blocks,
  And, reckoned in brain-hours,
When she outgrows her bobbysocks
  She starts on whiskey sours.

O consommé of gas-balloons,
  Whoopsdearie of them all!
A town of seven million goons
  Behind the octave ball.

Of what avail her towers high
  If in them men devote
Their minds to trivial things? But I
  Should worry! (End of quote.)

Avaunt, old bag! (Himself replied)
  Pipe down, and cut the squawk.
Your remarks are much too snide
  About N'Yawk, N'Yawk.

You bet, her tastes are corny:
  The public's always are;
And I may end my journey
  In some unritzy bar,

But, in the final ember,
  Discriminate am I;
From boyhood I remember
  Diana in the sky,

When life was all for learning
  (The top of human time!)
And mind was full of morning,
  And language burst with rhyme.

Now, when my hours are shortened,
  Fresh music I would bring;
She gives me, when disheartened,
  Magnificence to sing—

The song of smart connivers,
  Of crowded subway stops,
Of tough old taxi-drivers
  And much-enduring cops,

The ancient Down Town Fever,
  The smell of ferry slips,

And always and forever
　　The pageant of her ships.

Unroll me then this mappamond
　　Of all the life men know,
Grotesque and arabesque beyond
　　The Tales of Edgar Poe.

And though she tear my mind in two
　　In joy and pity split,
I love her; and so Nuts to You—
　　It's *my* mind, isn't it?

New York, New York!—Two moods betwixt,
　　Half fearful and half fain
(O love, O anger, always mixed!)
　　He got aboard the train.

Elegy in a Railroad Station

(Broad Street, Philadelphia, obiit 1952)

I've always been in love with railroad stations:
By no means least of man's superb creations.
Particularly I rate high
Old London termini,
Liverpool Street (cathedral of catarrh)
Where antique bathtubs in the cellar are;
And you may know
Altars of the great gods To and Fro
At Paddington, Euston, King's Cross, Gare du Nord,
La Salle Street in Chicago, Windsor Montreal,
The Lackawanna on Hoboken shore,
The B & O beloved Mount Royal, Baltimore.
Even little Roslyn, on fish-shaped Paumanok,
Where the Long Island falters, still in hock—
Too many I love, to list, but of them all
None ever gave me quite such sublimation
As Broad Street Station.
Maybe tops of all I rank it
Because it was there, by jeepers,
Walt climbed aboard the Pullman Palace Sleepers
And tucked his noble beard outside the blanket.

I repeat your glory, Broad Street Station!
The proper shrine, the true Main Line,
Of Immortality the Intimation;
Such offsteam blowing,
Such bells, and hells of coming and going,
Suburban cowcatchers' dainty snouts,
Beautiful barytone *All abooaard* shouts,
Drive wheels, and firebox glowing.
Nothing was so holy as the Local to Paoli

(15 and 45) when we were youngalive
For Wynnewood, Ardmore, Haverford, Bryn Mawr
Or anywhere along the P.R.R.
Then, as child, boy, student, family man,
We were too self-occupied to scan
That gigantic arch of joys and pains
When trains were really trains.

There beneath tall wheels, fierce jets of steam,
We guessed the bulk and power of a dream;
To shorten space and anguish to appease
The engine rests at crouch and purrs at ease.
People cry God bless you's and So long's,
Gates contract or widen like lazy-tongs—
Goodbye, Goodbye! No wonder I
Preserve in pure imagination
My memory of Broad Street Station.

All Passion and Publicity Spent

Our "Lyrical Ballads" may be due early in the Twentieth Century.
        —-George Saintsbury (1896)
The writers of today have not been born into a happy age for poetry.
        —Lord David Cecil (1941)

Every age is happy for happy poets
Who learn to bypass horrors of the day.
Saintsbury, old scintillate supreme,
Had scarce approved his Scottish-printed galleys
When fresh youth, Housman and Stephen Phillips
Were new-acclaimed the newest of all great.
Myself, I think the likely "Lyrical Ballads,"
The preview (dry-run?) of our shambled verse,
Were Gerard Hopkins, outgive in '18,
Or wry-on-rocks Tom Eliot, about then,
And our tart wrinklewit from Tennessee,
John Crowe Ransom. Not so Greekish he
As Stephen Phillips braw in cricket flannels.
Phillips moaned like Keats's god in pain
And blew his top in frolic. You remember
He tweaked Colvin's butler by the tails
(Coat-tails that is) to erb another drink.
It was Colvin told me.

How would you remember? Your taste in arts
Is subdivisioned in publicity.
Reread old Saintsbury? (I doubt you will)
And see wine-vinegar subfuse the oil.

Forty years past I saw, personal-saw,
The Muse turn over on her other cheek
When Henry James and Bridges took their bow
Among the rabbitskins and scarlet hoods.

I was one of the earliest modernists
Before we guessed (in 1912!) that we were "modern."
Before Yale, Rutgers, Florida press releases
We only dreamed our pitiable sooth. . . .

So then, To hell with John-come-late reviewers,
Resume, refresh the veteran professor;
Five times diddled for his Fellowship
Pricked him to such gianthood of effort.
I choose his briny-bearded semi-statement
And cast our gaping mussels on the beach.
With me, half-said is all I choose to say;
And know what *not* to say (divine iambic)
In the intense seclusion of the mind.

All passion spent, and all publicity,
My telephone not numbered in the book,
Nowhere will you find a happier man.
All birds are redbreast in the setting sun.

Death of a Talesman

Dja ever see such a wonderful sky?

No, not I.

Pure clouds adrift with silver purfle,
Blanched and flapped in northwest laundering!

I should be cheerful?
You're maundering.

Beshrew me, in such frosty air
You should be there
And cast your shout for God's Grand Jury,
With glory and with fury smitten—

Excuse me, but I daren't go out:
There's poetry everywhere
Still unwritten.

Climacteric

In younger days our poems just foamed over,
Bursting biology like boiling milk;
Seeded at large as ragweed and red clover,
Not winkled with a pin, like a cockney whelk.
Wordsworth, rutting-seasoned as a rabbit,
Kept breeding verse far past the daffodil,
But Coleridge, undisciplined in habit,
Went silent by paralysis of will.

Oh silence, eloquent silence! for whose joys
We shake the ecstasies of Hot Pursuit
And switch swift alcohols for lazy wine.
Like Santayana, flunk the Harvard boys
Where cheek by cheek we ripen our own fruit,
One sonnet more on the Dissembly Line.

I Knew a Country——

I knew a country bushed with to-and-fro,
Where paperwork might pyramid success;
Where tickertapes all rattled, Yes, yes, yes!
And Top Bananas, half-ripe, grumbled No!
The Bicarb Party, burping Maybe so,
Dividing stress by strain, or strain by stress,
Were griped like Hamlet, for they could not guess
TV or not TV, by video.

It takes fatigue and savvy, pain and grace,
And more than supermarket reach and span
To carve new character on a nation's face.
Men yearned for it, from high or humble place,
While down the flume the foaming hours ran—
What country?
          The Country without a Man.

Madrigal Not to Be Reprinted
I, too, have tried to be modern.—W. B. Yeats (1935)

When your mood is joy
Give out with a shout, bully-boy:
Riotous, pink as a child from sleep,
Eyes burning Saxon-blue
Let the rabble share with you
And babble, and applaud it.
Laughter needs audit.

But if (it might be tomorrow)
You are despair,
Then secret keep; quiet creep
Into your sorrow.
There you live alone,
Breech and bone and marrow.
Retire, retreat, repair,
Immurable in your lair.

Defeat no company will bear,
No consort, hide nor hair,
Sorrow wants no one there,
Not anyone, anywhere.

Britain for the Holidays

I

The emblems of a British holiday
Outwitting the austerities of Cato
Are the raincoat not too far away,
Potato and potato and potato.
The tiny car, rebuilt, is 'running in';
Chop cabbage and smoke haddock and steam kipper,
Invoke the sausage with the vellum skin
That ought to be provided with a zipper.

Great Britain queues up for an hour of sun;
Never basked so many in hours so few,
Nowhere so many parked wrongside; drive slow!
Bless pleasure-hungry Britons, every one,
And grant them, so good-humoredly in queue,
Their acme of approval: *Not a bad show.*

II

The Island Race, set forth on leg and wheel,
Likes what it knows, and knows just what it likes:
Plenty of mustard on its ham-and-veal;
Not open roads, but those well filled with bikes.
Pack in enduring infants, ditto dogs.
At temperatures of seventy-plus they sizzle,
And if belike there happen rains and fogs
These are accepted as refreshing drizzle.

Prepare the buns-and-butter, the fish fritter!
And, as goal and goblet of adventures,
The brimming mugs of tepid mild-and-bitter

To rinse the busy governmental dentures.
Wrapped in oilskins, under dripping trees,
A stalwart people seek 'amenities.'

III

Admit, Britannia has 'bright intervals'—
One slice of sun, as thin as buttered crust,
Mosses are emerald mice on roofs and walls,
She sheds her muffles, yearns to be untrussed.
But aspen lifts white petticoats to the gust:
The glass percussed, it steadies? No, it falls.
Britannia robes again, proving as she must
Connoisseur of climate; scholar of squalls.

Here in a royal seigniory of oak
Watching clouds that sag uncertainly
I smell the southwest in sweet cottage-smoke
And think it prudent to stay in for tea.
Britain, sun-and-rainshot till she spangles,
Has been tough education for the Angles.

IV

I saw three swans in Friday sunset flying;
Evening's golden lances pierced the wood;
Lawn and cricket field were slowly drying;
Meseemed the meteorology was good.
There was a rainbow showing the full prism,
Weatherwise Girl Guides were pitching camp;
My ankles were not grieved with rheumatism,
Even bedroom sheets were hardly damp.

I dined, and answered with a keen digestion
The familiar treble-British question

Thick or clear? sweet, savoury? black or white?
Orion glittered cap-à-pie that night.
Everything was Ticking Over.—Then
The morn, and the morn's morn, it rained again.

V

And now we settle for the autumn drowse:
The bee, snapdragon-trapped, turns in and snores;
Dogs idle in mid-scratch; men gape like cows.
Ripeness is all. Lethargy is outdoors.
By harvest-shaven fields the old blue bus
At cottages and farm-lanes tremble-stopping,
Missus heaves aboard, mornings all of us
Who trundle in to Lymington for shopping.

Tiles are newly gilt with pats of lichen,
Window-plants and dahlias are ablaze,
Plum-and-wasp is boiling in the kitchen,
Oilywoite is Tennysonian haze—
And I remember, bumping on the road,
It was in Hampshire that Keats wrote the Ode.

VI

Poets are always foreigners; they see clear
In the lens of other poets' eyes:
What half-familiar flowers to recognize,
What durable trees; birds with accents, hear!
Visit and search, enchantment multiplies:
The mortal miracle is very near
When alien weather under alien skies
Is equally rare, and commonplace, and dear.

The English oak is packed with acorns still
While Paumanok seres in yellow, pink, and rust.

Whence and wherever love's contagion grew,
We dream of kindred anguish to fulfill:
Keats sickened here; Hardy breathed cider-must;
There are the leaves of grass Walt Whitman knew.

Hampshire, August–September 1951.

Unborn Poem

Oh delicate in the middle night
Between the floor and ceiling
I have an anxious feeling,
By a feeling I am smitten,
That some time soon I'll maybe write
    Rather, there will write itself
A poem that wants to be written.

Poem-germ, so infinitesimal,
You might yet be a Dewey Decimal:
Yo-heave-ho, kick, help yourself
If you want to live on the Open Shelf.
    I'll try too. You've the best of me
    If I assume nonentity.
    If you or I are hurried or worried
    By shall's and will's, or who'd and whom'd,
    Unwritten poem, then you're doomed.

I knew an unborn poem
Who dreamed about all the professors
Who'd want to reprint him freely dative
In textbooks about Process Creative.
He suffered from prenatal shrivel;
When he was born he was only drivel.
    I'm taking a deep hot bath, long soakable,
    I won't try to think a single vocable.
    I'll trim my nails; I'll read a book;
    Let Beauty strip, I won't even look;
    Venus appear from her purple billow,
    My head is modestly under the pillow.
Oh god or goddess, rise and shine,
I must help in your way, not in mine.

Then, when minuscule hours were coming,
Insufferable joy he hears!
Is it the harmony of the spheres,
Or the precessions of the years?
Or some stillicide in the plumbing?
The endless rhythm, whisper-drumming:
The terror, lonely as life can make it:
Satan saying 'you can't take it.'
> *Now, by Trunnion and by Trulliber,*
> *My wrist is dripping the sword Excalibur;*
> *The English prof., a bull of Bashan,*
> *Says this is Guilt by Association—*
But strong I feel, however queer,
I'll find it written on paper here:
Frolic maybe? Freak or skit?
This is evidently not it—
But still it's early . . . . listen . . . . say!
It might happen Today.

Of an Ancient Spaniel in Her Fifteenth Year

She was never a dog that had much sense,
Too excitable, too intense,
But she had the cocker's gift of charm.
She never knew what to do with a bone,
But shielded all her life from harm
She cost me several years of my own.

Sweet old pooch! These final years
She rubs white chaps and floating ears
In summersweet suburban loam;
Digs, she thinks, a final home:
Scoops every day fresh graves to lie,
Humble and contented, knowing
Where, any day now, she'll be going—
And so do I.

I said, buying with Christmas care,
Her collar and tag for '49:
This is the last she'll ever wear
(And the same is true of mine).
Equal mercy, and equal dark
Await us both, eternally,
But I was always ready to bark—
And so was she.

And a Crooked Tree

An evening star, and a crooked tree
Are clarified on dusk for me;
And I, who have scarce energy
My private verse to copy fair,
Am frost-consumed in vesper air.

But what of the world and I not there?
Do I really care?
I had good advice for men's despair:
You can find it exactly where
I said it. Most of it's o.p.*

Yes, I shall miss you terribly,
My evening star and my crooked tree,
When Orion, isosceles, angled right,
Comes tilting northward through the night.
* Out of print.

Death of a Poet

Once, the Great Lyric blazed inside his head:
He saw the flame, he felt the heat—and fled.
Power was gone. Too long, too many times
He had depleted all his strength in rhymes.

Obit for Aunt Nev (M.V.M.)

I knew a grand old wench
  Who had worked full hard and sore:
    On the first warm day
    She would always say
I'd like to lie down on an alehouse bench
  And snore . . . . and snore.

Gentlemen's Relish
(After rereading *Autolycus in Limbo*, by Vincent Starrett)

I've been rereading poems by V. S.
With their delicious tang of mustard-and-cress
And "Gentlemen's Relish" (*patum peperium*)
Which shops don't have, no matter how you query 'em.
To stew this down to a sonnet, I'd be lief,
But, frankly, I've no time to be brief.

Vincenzio! with just less than a laugh
You used to wonder about your epitaph,
And hope, perhaps like Beerbohm's "Enoch Soames,"
To live as footnote in great bibliotomes.
Like all the poets (bless them) that I know
Whose oils and vinegars have pleased me so,
Your golden mind, medallioned in the mint
Of sometimes very much too private print,
Is also varicose with highblue blood.
Let others bake their fashion-pies in mud:
Us, till the zipper jams in the brain-suture,
Let's capitalize the future.
Lionel Johnson had the word, when dead:
Haud minimus habebitur the stoic tablet said.

But poets need to be told
Before they get too old:
Time runs A to Izzard,
And before the gizzard
Is full of blizzard
And mortal arteries flow thick, or thin,
Toast them a slog of gin;
They who have griddled their souls

To serve you verse-casseroles,
Need wine from the Rib of Gold (Côte d'Or)
Or juleps, and crabs, from Baltimore
Or sweetbreads sous clôche, by the plateful,
To show them how you're grateful
For ecstasies you hadn't had before.

Be technical! Tell him you set your heart in youth on
His off-rhythm, or his anacoluthon,
His heavy spondee, his iamb, or trochee,
All, by Coleridge, were okey-dokey—
Or you think, to be blunt, he is probably best
In the leap and the bound of the swift anapaest
But also suggest
He supplement the concave of his vest
With an additament of antipasto
In gurgite vasto,
Then, if he knows the score, he
Will order chicken cacciatore.

Well-and-truly gruntle! Pour something stiff in
The forepeak of your hospitable tiffin,
And tell him then (as if he didn't know it)
The maigritude of some competing poet
Or editor: it was the poet's amphibology
Made him all too subtle for the new anthology.
Such little skillet-fry of crumbs and crappie
Can make a poet happy.
Twirl on the penpoint, like a tipskate dancer,
You'll get an answer.
Once I wrote a poet how his double-entendre
Had made me ponder:
The frolic mischief of his double meanings

Had married and got meanings of their own—
He wrote (in holograph) that after all desk-cleanings
I was the only critic he'd ever known.

But do it now: before the Angel with the sponge
Makes his all-obliterating plunge;
Do it, in typefounders' caps and serifs,
As the oldtime Oxford kitchen tariffs
Said "Gentlemen's own birds cooked and served":
Yea, stuff, bake, piecrust the elusive bird
And sauce with onion-sage and breaded curd
And relish until trivial taste has swerved.
Do it! Myself, I always told them
Before the afterbell had knolled them,
And saw, in many agonies they wrote,
What the hereafter won't have wit to quote.

Vincenzio! You know as well as I
To you and me, of course, this don't apply:
But just for luck, among our private words,
"Gentlemen's Relish"—"Gentlemen's Own Birds."
    Poetry, we've learned, can not be sold,
    But poets still have hunger To Be Told:
    They coin their livers and their lights in mint
    But Zeus Himself can't keep their stuff in print.

Interruptions (an Essay in Verse)

Shakespeare, going good, in a working dream:—
> *The cloudcapped towers, the gorgeous palaces,*
> *The solemn temples, the great globe itself,*
> *Yea—dissolve—inherit—*
There comes a scream:
> Will, hither! Bestir thee, Will!
> (The man's a loon, I swear it)
> Dost naught about the house?
> Come to the aid of thy spouse,
> There's a mouse on the larder shelf
And the cat's upset the cream!

Happily combing his beard with an inky quill,
> Drinking port in seidels,
Tennyson deemed all else was nil
> But elegies and idylls:—
> *Tears from the depth of some divine despair—*
But from the top of the stair
Sounds the sudden scare, and shrill:
> Hurry up, Alf! Your Emily
> Is going to have more family;
> Beat feet and do your share,
> Tear up some old soft underwear,
> Bring towels and hot water—
You've got another daughter.

Or Jefferson, on Independence bent:
> *We hold these truths self-evident—*
> *Life—Liberty—unalienable right—*
The patriot soul, in concentration whole,
Is making notes, for a thousand years of quotes—
> Tom! You Tom! yells feminine lament;

And then, in a fit of the vapors:
    Leave off those silly old papers,
The dogs are in a fight.

Maybe Goethe, steaming on his *Faust*
In a comfortable frowst,
In the twentieth year on the Second Part
Coming near the dream of his heart
Heard someone open the door, and roar:
    Wolf! Gottes Willen, oeffnet das Fenster!
    Lass fliegen die Gespenster!
That passage was irretrievably loused,
    And he always held it against her.

The great Professor Stubbs, at Christmas '73,
Writing the preface to his History
(A masterpiece of jurisprudence,
Forgotten by most but Oxford students)—
    The worst cause has often been illustrated
    With the most heroic virtue—
But his mind is dissipated
When he hears the children bawl
In the home in Kettel Hall:—
    The goose is on the table and we're starving;
    Hi, Daddy! Regius Prof.!
    It's time for scoff,
    Come and do the carving!

There is one horror makes all writers kin,
Drives them to stomach ulcers or to gin:
Interruption, their poor alibi
For not writing things that never die.

But even more ridiculous and sad,
Those who lived so sheltered that they never had
Domestic uproar, or a telephone call,
Were never heard of at all.

Grandpa Sings to Himself

Who else has sat so many evenings late
When feet and yells subsided overhead,
Brooding on the briefness of estate
And simple pities that he might have said.
It would be sad if we procrastinate
These openings of heart until we're dead,
But prosody is hard to calibrate
Till everybody else is put to bed.

Then, elderly, distempered, and absurd,
With plentiful anxieties to worry,
He is as lively at the written word
As Pope-on-Thames, or Meredith in Surrey.
CROMPA (as they call him) finds it good,
And would he live it all again? He would.

Winter Moon

In the clear inkwell of tonight,
Embayed in rolling silver scud,
A floating Athens, marble-bright,
Rules the republics of the blood.

Beshrew her then! So say we all
Who perish in our septuagint:
Permit one mortal caterwaul,
One molten stick of human print.

Scotch-granite as the Stone of Scoon,
Numb State Department in the sky,
Barren with protocol—Oh Moon,
One final toast, before we die:—

Never creator, mere consumer,
The moon, who has no sense of humor.

Too Long I Loitered

Too long I loitered in dismay
Where word-crammed silences divide
The heart from what it craves to say.
The snow was caked northside the tree
And I was bored to death with Me.
I had no song, I had no pride,
And growing old, and terrified.

Then late of more than sixty springs
Came plain language unforeboded,
Speech that needed no rehearse:
Just in time the curse exploded,
Shattered black imaginings,
And music canceled in one verse
A million hours of trivial things.

Morning After

After such long busywork of dying
It was so peaceful in the stratosphere
I wondered, am I going to be bored?
Then old Peter Pearlygate, replying:
"Gosh sake, I never thought to see *you* here;
You'll have to wait a while to see The Lord."
He scanned his book. "You got the breaks, old boy.
While your attendant Angel rests, and combs
His plumage—he looks a little ruffled—
Take it easy. What would you most enjoy?"

I said: To learn again how words, well shuffled,
Can sort miraculously into rhyme;
Or better still, read as for the first time
One of the Adventures of Sherlock Holmes.

Consolation

(Carl Sandburg: *Always the Young Strangers*, p. 92)

Man made his own hell, now there's hell to pay.
Treble-weary, head and heart and hand,
I shrink from daily outrage and dismay
Willful beyond my scope to understand.
Man's misery, I thought, is too immense
For my alleviation, even pity:
Let me withdraw to private impotence,
In mind alone is our Eternal City.

Then, Carl, old friend, I chance this day to read
Your chronicle of youth, in which you say
Once in a Galesburg morning very early
You told your Old Man, that tough honest Swede,
"Some of those stars are millions of miles away."
"Ve von't bodder about dat yust now, Sharlie!"

It Will Last My Time

I tried my mind to quiet
  With verses mixed or plain,
But now that I have nothing
  For losing, or for gain,
I whisper you my secret,
  My private gin-and-lime—
  It will last my time.

They tell me space collapses
  Till rockets travel soon
By planet-platforms mooring
  For journeys to the moon.
I've done my share of roaming
  By wheel and keel and climb—
  It will last my time.

New verses shall be written
  (I hear) in braver mode,
And no one dreams attempting
  The rondeau, or the ode:
I loved all kinds of poems,
  Some even were in rhyme—
  It will last my time.

They say love will be richer,
  Fresh passions deeper move:
Bushwa! if I remember,
  Myself invented love!
Thank God, such wealth of loving
  I've had since early prime—
  It will last my time.

Grammarian's Funeral in Hurricane Weather

This is the kind of weather that we get
When there's hurricane in the Bahamas;
Folks don't perspire, they (Anglo-Saxon) sweat,
There's mould on books and fungus on pajamas.
Now postage stamp adheres to postage stamp,
The envelope gums up the letter-meter,
The paper match is limp, and static damp
Even almost muffles Gabriel Heatter.

On such a day our Old Grammarian went,
Disgusted with the whole curriculum;
As he lay raving in the oxygen tent
The sputum cup obediently he spat in,
But young science profs were stricken dumb
To hear him die, growling *Study Latin!*

Self-Unmade Man, or The Graduate
of the Great Books Course

He read all the wise men and maximeers
And double-checked their text for years.

From Socrates to Pearsall Smith
He found all aphorists had pith,
Even sometimes Meredith.

Vauvenargues he pronounced as cloven,
Meaning, this way argues Vauven;
He wondered who was Chrysoprase,
Philosopher of ancient days?

Swiftly as a flying saucer
He skims empyrean Chaucer;
Then, in application dutiful,
Burke on the Sublime and Beautiful;
And, happily confused, combines
Waldo Emersons, Waldo Trines.

Ecclesiastes and Voltaire;
La Rochefoucauld and La Bruyère
(These, he thought, both ladies were)
And, to add more manly power,
Schopenhauer, Eisenhauer.
Marquis, Mencken, or Montaigne,
Ogden Nash or Thomas Paine,
All to his earnest mill were grist
If mentioned on a Reading List.

How wise he must become by now,
You say. I also wonder how

After reading these Great Works
He still is plunder for all jerks.
I wouldn't leave him alone at night
With a lawyer, or a traffic light.

Secrets of the Library

One literary problem shook
  Both teacher and progenitor:
The youth who will not read a book
  Unless he's read the book before.
My boy, my compliment to you;
I feel exactly that way too.

Memory of a Sheepdog

When he was young, and combed, he was quite a curly-dog;
When he grew old he was rather a surly-dog.

He dreamed no more chickens to chivvy, or phantom sheep;
All he wanted (all anyone wants) is sleep.

He was full of aches he knew not how to tell,
Matted with prickleburrs his dear old fell,

That long exhaling sigh (a crumbling tooth?)
Was hairy Falstaff in a Blue Boar booth.

Years (they seemed longer) he had barkaloo to explode
At midnight on our terrified country road,

But when, beyond such prowess in the garth,
He would lie warming, as he thought, the hearth

He would still, apologetically, avail
When you walked over, to flap his heavy plumy tail.

Now I think things past, I don't know any
Companion won my homage more than Donny.

It isn't easy to die with dignity—
No one ever did more honorably than he.

Even with growls, I relish life coming up:
Even in children; even in a pup.

Richness of Life

Length comes on the days,
And my tall tulip trees
Twinkle at the top.
So now, with summer climbing,
I reckon up my joys.

My richest asset
Is my excitable neighbor
To whom I told my favorite story
About Kipling and the White Elephant
At the Zoo in Regent's Park.
"You mean to say," cried my friend,
"The Elephant really embraced him
With his probiscus?"

Frogs and Squirrels

The moon is not so far away
  Above my favorite crooked tree,
Where greenbud-hungry squirrels sway
  In empty April tracery.

The frogs, in my mudhumble swamp,
  Are whistlingales of boyhood joy;
But squirrels only grind and chomp,
  And care not how much they destroy.

As Keats once said, in a wonderful letter,
I've written a poem . . . I feel better.

Fourfootnote for "Modern Love"

I love to think
How furious George Meredith was
When he sat down
In the belvedere on Box Hill
To write a sonnet.
No one else was so persistent about sonnets
As to stretch them to 16 lines.

But when the famous English critic
Told us that Meredith was infatuated with dachshunds
It was Florida Weisscracker
(The poet of the Great Dismal Swamp)
Who screamed: Now I know
Why his sonnets were two lines too long.

Cornerstone for McFadden's Flats

Men and women, in one flat,
Lead the life of dog and cat.

Oh architect, a flight of stairs
Proximity and temper spares.

Avoid, my dears, contiguous devils
And grind your teeth on different levels.

Let each, in privacy apart,
Wring the withers, purge the heart.

Only so, and unprofaned,
Is your flatlet self-contained.

The Razor's Edge

Since the most broadcast reports
Of our national sports
Have a razor for sponsor
(The world's most prosperous tonsor)
I think it unethical and craven
That a bearded man unshaven,
A man whose jowls are never barbered
Either port or starboard,
A man on whom blades never glisten,
Should listen.

To my shame, with hairy chin,
I tune in.

A Mother's Day Poem in Memory of
My Mother, Who Cared Very
Little for Mother's Day

My mother (and God rest her gallant soul)
    Dictated me a prayer when I was young:
"Pray the Lord to help you to control
    Your temper, your excitement, and your tongue."

That petition, at my mother's knee,
Was, I hope, good discipline for me—
And yet I've rarely known full ecstasy
Except when I have let them rip, all three.

Inscription for a Boiled Shirt

Truth
Is often uncouth.

A lie, for politesse,
Wears evening dress
And with all its faults
Is graceful as a waltz.

Good Housekeeping

To throw away three inches of candle
Is, to my habit of thought, a scandal.
Who burns the taper down to the socket
Will always have small change in pocket,
And a light, which he uses
When storms blow fuses.

Birdmaster General

Our neighborhood is overcrowded
With ornithology.
I had to abandon
My R.F.D. mailbox
Because the P.O. and the birds
Were always deadlocked for possession.

Why doesn't the Postmaster General
Invent a double-ended box,
One side for the double-breasted mockingbird
And the other for the mail?

Sonnet on Copyright
(For Melville Cane and Max Chopnick)

There were two kinds of sonnets: *Whenas I*,
Or *As One Who*; and both were egotism;
But I should hope to write one, full and bye,
In the lighter colors of the prism.

I love them all, from Ronsard to Rossetti,
So syllabled in sable for the sibyl,
But mine, if I may toss my own confetti,
Will be at least, I pray, intelligible.

Of course it must have ambience of its own
(The critic-word in fashion nowadays)
But leave its foot and vestige on the stone
Like that Euclidean sandal of Millay's.

And it will be, or else the law is nix,
Copyright, until 2-0-0-6.

The New Housemaid
(Christmas 1894)

This 'ere's a blinkin' place, 221-B:
You carn't do nothink right, blimey, because
'Oo wants when, and what? Cawfee? Early tea?
Rashers? At nine, snoring a treat they was,
Now 'Olmes's bath's too cold, Doctor's too 'ot;
Their eggs is boiling solid in the shell.
'Ow do you twig 'om's 'om, and when, and wot?
But Mrs. 'Udson says . . .
      Oh Gord, the Bell!
House, lodgers, maid, all gone. The pavement's there
Which hansom, growler, even royal brougham
Scraped in hot haste for desperate appeals.
Baker Street, your memorial is where
On the way to the consulting room
This was the kerb that ground a thousand wheels.

Orion Bears His Pack

Outdoor my kitchen steps he wambles on,
The hugest hobo pattern of our sky:
Sirius, Betelgeuse, and Procyon
Are corners of the pack he bears so high—
A burden any bindlestiff to crack:
I marvel for him, evenings of clear show,
Heaving still, on overtoppled back,
The cumbered bottomless bag of human woe.

But rank imposes heavy stars on shoulders:
He sags, he vanishes down westbeyond,
Whistled and cheered by neutralist beholders
And fluting freshman frogs in Gissing Pond.
His cosmic rucksack, overload of earth,
Cinched tight, and three-star-buckled at the girth.

Sun-Dial Motto Offered to but Not Accepted by a Women's College

In every college, even Smith,
Error must be reckoned with.
Your time is Daylight? Then do well with it.
I say it's Greenwich, and to hell with it.
The truth, in bronze as well as ink:
Girls, you're younger than you think.

Ours Was an Age (1900–1950)

Ours was an age when poets wept
   And innocence went under;
And every conscience cleanly kept
   Cries out, it is no wonder.

Ours was an age in pain consumed,
   In crowds, and haste mechanic;
To fever and frustration doomed
   It consummates in panic.

Ours was an age of jigs and gears
   When science was heroic;
A golden age for engineers,
   But, for us weaker, stoic.

Ours was an age when sky's pure breath,
   In which the mind rejoices,
Men used to talk themselves to death
   With contradicting Voices.

Hickory and Honeysuckle

There's a fable in my garden
Sometimes helps my heart to harden,
Where a stripling hickory tree
Straight as any growth may be
Was embraced in deadly twine
By a honeysuckle vine.

Hickory its hope pursued,
Every spring the fight renewed,
But the suffocating sweetness
Every spring with more completeness
Winds a tourniquet entangled.
Hickory will soon be strangled,
Now begins to fade and buckle—
Victory for honeysuckle.

Many years I watched the pair,
Mutually murderous there.
What's the moral *you* would draw
From the struggle that I saw?
Tell me not! A studying man
Keeps Nature's secrets, if he can.

Personal

Just as I was leaving for my vacation
I was embarrassed to see
An advertisement
At the Neighborhood Men's Shop:—

SUMMER CLEARANCE
OF SLACKS AND LOAFERS.

Unhandy

Let each day be your textbook, someone said:
There is as much truth here as anywhere.
A straw revolving on a spider-thread
Tutors me the physics of hot air;
In mouldy cheese, or speckle-staling bread
I calculate new penicillins there.

Theoretically a good learner,
I must have mastered what I need to know
About a noncombustible oil-burner,
A vacuum cleaner, stove, or radio.
My small demesne, according to my story,
Tells every scientific ipse-dixit—
But something goes wrong in this laboratory?
I have to hire a better man to fix it.

Flying Saucers

Those Lubbock Lights, green fireballs, flying saucers
That pass at supersonic speeds and vanish,
Leave not a rack behind; only a dim
Geiger-count of burning mathematics,
A shimmer evanescent on the night. . . .

I can tell you, says the Old Mandarin,
What are those interplanetary memoes:
They are my little poems, cinder fragments
That cruised the sky a moment, and left only
A nose besulphured and a breath of burning;
Like John Aubrey's ghost, in 1670,
"A curious perfume and melodious twang."

They disappeared, says Old Felicity,
Into the paradise called Out-of-Print.

Rude Brief Recitatives
(For Walt Whitman's 134th Birthday)

IN 1955

During Ike's Presidentiad
It would be fine if somewhere in Washington
(Maybe at the Library of Congress)
A small tablet were imposed:
Shut not your doors to me, proud libraries.

BHANG!

Oriental mystics are always harsh
To the mystics of the West.
When I cajoled the Old Mandarin
To the multiplex musings of "Leaves of Grass"
He grumbled only:
This is corned-beef hashish.

TOWARD THE END

Walt was probably the only great writer
Who never owned a bookcase
Or even a filing cabinet.
He filed everything on the floor
And edited with the tip of his cane.
When Traubel rescued priceless letters
He found them "much trodden."
Old screwball Walt! But he did save
Little orbic tangles of string
Which sometimes got into Mrs. Davis's soup
And were eaten for noodles.

CUPPING AND LEECHING

When he trimmed his hair and beard
With his own blunt scissors

It caused more sensation in Washington
Than the battle at Gettysburg.
The only artisans
With whom Walt never got folksy
Were barbers.

THE OTHER ONE WAS BOOTH

Walt, whom I have studied
More patiently than most,
Spent the last twenty years in South Jersey,
Between the Pine Barrens and the Brain Barrens.
Like every Victorian actor
He saw America as a pantomime
And viewed it through a scrim.

HIS HOLIDAY

His naïveté was so vast, so hugeous,
It was a gigantism, an elephantiasis.
He glorified the Open Road
But kept well off of it.
He loved ferries and buses
Where he could chant unheard.
The day he chose was the busman's holiday
When he could crack the whip
And someone else stabled the horses.
Every married man knows
Walt always skipped the homework.

OTHERS HE SHAVES

Briefly and bitterly, then,
Walt was never housebroken.
Santayana, the other most selfish solipsist,
Even at his Blue Nuns, shaved every day.

❧ 78 ❧

No wonder he called Walt
A barbarian.

MY ESCAPE

I used to be sorry
That several years I worked near Horace Traubel
I never called on him—
But how it cheers me
When I learn from those who did
What an appalling bore he was—
And so perhaps was Walt?

BETWEEN TIMES

Not even the critics,
Not even Walt,
Have had as much fun and firework
Out of his stuff as I.
Cautiously I only read him from time to time
But between those times
I find myself thinking about him.

SAY IT AGAIN

When Willie Yeats said (1936)
In his essay for
"The Oxford Book of Modern Verse"
That a poem should rise
Out of its own rhythm,
He was only saying what our instinctive old Walt
Said again and again to his ignorant discipules
While the guttersnipes of Camden
Yelled one-old-cat on the cobbles of Mickle Street
And the guano factory near-by
Was more potent, in those days,
Than Campbell's savory Tomato.

PAY-OFF

If Walt reaches another end-of-May
I might have more to say,
Maybe veal-cutlets, maybe pudding-batter;
But in what don't really matter
Walt (and I) are both like Dante—
Pococurante.

Dachshund Nextdoor

For years exactly thirty-three
I've lived on this my property,
And kept my bounds, and paid my tax.

My neighbor has a brand new dachs
Who doesn't yet quite understand
The facts of ownership in land,
And when my limits I patrol
Expostulates with bark and howl.

Oh dachshund, allerkleinsten Bruder,
Who bark at *me* as an intruder!
If God walked earth again, I fear
Man cries "Hey! Watcha doin' here?"

Shakespeare in Junior High

I'm reading Shakespeare, Fourteen Years confessed:
*He's tops! I don't suppose in Junior High
We get it all: but gee, I like him best
When he writes about Me. He makes me cry!
Could I say that, in my English test?*

Say it; and you, musicians of the spheres,
Know that your glory never was so great
As when our humble parallel appears,
And in the Universal agony
You recognize, condone, and sublimate
The all-devouring all-transmuting Me.

Bespeak us when we were savage, young, and pure:
When we lived, not studied, literature:
Sonnets not fourteen lines, but fourteen years.

Wasting Shakespeare's Time

On my Grand Climacteric
(When I entered my 63rd year)
I was showing the Old Mandarin
A shelf of books I had written.

I think he was quite surprised.
After all, I said, in self-defense,
I've lived ten years longer than Shakespeare did.

His remark was razor:
If only Shakespeare could have had
Those extra ten years.

The Apes

One evening when the apes
(My private love-name for grandchildren)
Wouldn't eat their supper,
I said in despair,
Well, let's put the children in the icebox,
And put the rice pudding to bed.

They thought this was really funny:
They shrilled with laughter:
Poor babes, it was their first experience
Of amphibology.
Or was it oxymoron?

150th Anniversary of the Edinburgh Review

The *Edinburgh Review*
Was founded in 1802.
In every college seminar
Its best-known words still are
This will never do.
The truth (as students say, no kid)
Is, it never did.

Except the author, what men love most
Is a real ribroast,
A barbecue.

The *Edinburgh* was full of spine,
And it went down the drain lang syne,
But even old and tired and shabby
I'll probably re-read *Tintern Abbey.*

The Sub-Imago

"The water is crystal clear
And good for the nymph,"
Says the instruction for anglers
At a village well-named Hook.
"Trout of aldermanic proportions . . . .
A devotee of the sub-imago."

A day with the dry fly,
A dusk with dry sherry,
The angler muses
Those trouts are not aldermen
But modernist poets.

Avant-Garde

If I could only make this
One great omnibus letter
To everyone I know!
But a whole new shepherds' pie
Of poetry and fiction and philosophy
Is now the compulsory fashion
And I haven't yet duly digested
The writers who were avant-garde
In the Nineteen-teens.

Every vanguard
Needs its own fanguard.
Every Papacy finds its bliss
In uniformed Swiss.

Birth of a Journalist

When my youngest grandson
Was one week old
He was taken with a luxurious burp
Which so shook him
That he opened his eyes to see what had happened
And reached out to try to catch it.

Dial Call

Deep calleth unto deep
(Said Psalm 42, vii)
But also shallow unto shallow
And gets more prompt reply.

Instrument Disconnected

If Wordsworth had had a telephone
It would have been answered by Dorothy.
If Doctor Johnson had had a telephone
It would have been answered by Yale University.
If Walt Whitman had had a telephone
It would never have been answered at all.

Autobiography

My large and liberal lassitude
Is not merely crassitude
I think of all I have loved best,
And play my thoughts close to my vest.

I give myself a sieve-and-screening,
Ask when-and-where-and-what had meaning?
So, frying in my private grease,
I am my own museum-piece.

Deny Everything

I often think,
Hurrying down the drive
To catch our one-a-day mailbox,
It was stupid I didn't learn to loaf
Till I was sixty-two.

If you learn too late,
No matter how lovingly you idle
There's no longer time to pay your neighbors
The compliments they deserve.
Your older neighbors have died of overwork,
The younger haven't grown up to loafing.

But, now I'm old enough to admit everything,
If they tell you I was a misanthrope
Or even a misogynist
Deny it please.

More Thoughts about Wordsworth

I like anthologies that note
The dates of poems that they quote.
If by noble verse I'm smitten,
I like to know when it was written.

I brew my secret wild perhapses
When half a century elapses
Between the writing and the print:
Could even Wordsworth take a hint?

Alas, in my own leaves-of-grassing
I know too well how time is passing.
What anguish took him by the throat? It
Helps to know what age he wrote it.

A *Birthday*
(Don Marquis, July 29, 1878)

Don, there was a time (not long away)
You gave us all our daily double-meaning,
A double-slug of wonder-drug:
The queen of cats went down the Bay
In a barge of garbage from street-cleaning,
And mounds of upperwestside refuse starchy
Were dietetic still for kingsize archy.

Down the Bay in a rubbage scow
To the dump off Scotland Light,
Toujours gai (miaow, miaow)
The tribe of Don are mostly gone
Blown higher than a kite.
But while our teeth were grittable
We ground them with mehitabel;
As long as our gooms were gnashable
Or our deposits cashable,
As long as we had carfare
We made psychological warfare
With archy, O king of vermin,
archy who could determine
everything uncertain
behind the ironical curtain.
He saw things from the under side,
But archy the roach was never snide.

What pungency lost all these years,
Quindecimal of hopes and fears
With comedy always in arrears!
Don was once our Secretary of State,
He, he only, would elucidate

Empiric sense, and grown-up men would say
Did you read Don's column yesterday?
I've known cabinet members who would snivel
If they could read those pieces now; and shrivel.

From Caedmon bashful in the byre
To O. Nash timid at the mike
The best of all our singing choir
Were unpredictably alike:
Some of their stuff was merely rhymes,
Then other times
They really drove the golden spike.

Our generation was not lost, but shent;
America has not laughed since archy went.
We, in this drouth of sweet midwestern corn
Crave glimpses that would make us less forlorn.
Enough of pansies and of pimpses,
We want glimpses
Of the Old Soak, of Red Haired Ladies,
Or mehitabel, the cat of Hades
Rising in death-dance from the D.S.C.
While old archy blows his dubious horn.
Bless oldtimers, who still praise and tell
The spacious days
Of archy and mehitabel.

Pennsylvania Deutsch

The rain it raineth every day
And freezeth as it raineth:
Old Grandpapa hath hell to pay,
His motor tire he chaineth.

The power-house constraineth,
The kilowatt eke waneth,
The countryside chilblaineth,
No calory remaineth.
Lhude sing kaput! The poor old coot
Indeed he is no malamute:
Already he hath shot the chute
And his ankle spraineth.

It raineth as it freezeth,
And every roadway greaseth:
Hark how Grandpa sneezeth.
Though the drive he salteth
United Parcels halteth;
Grandpa too much malteth,
His footing double-faulteth
And on the pavement vaulteth.
Lhude sing socko,
Grandpapa is crocko.

Northeast gale appalleth
And haileth as it squalleth,
But lo, the garbage calleth.
Like the great bird on bunions free
Grandpa comes forth busily,
Where the ice him loopeth
The kitchen steps him poopeth

He trieth to grab the banister,
He falleth on his canister.

On skull and double-rumpeth
The three-point landing bumpeth.
Now noodle-strudel soupeth
And congregation groupeth:
Deep from the neck they sing, deacons caterwaul,
Grandpapa is everything, Grandpa is all.
Lhude sing skiddo:
Grandma is a widow.

Classified

Among the Old Mandarin's well-loved protegés
Were a young couple who expected a baby.
Problems budgetary and midgetary
Were discussed.
Could we get, asked the hopeful O.M.,
Some rebate by Hospital Insurance?
Not a chance, groaned Young Spouse:
They classify pregnancy
As a Planned Illness.

Unfashionable

Poets in our civilization must be difficult—*T. S. Eliot, 1921*

In hope to please futurity,
Win critical security,
I strove to write obscurity,
    Said the Old Mandarin.

In spite of all acidity,
Humidity, morbidity,
Alas for me, lucidity
    Was always breaking in.

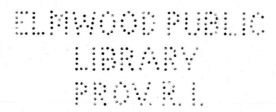
•§ 99 §•

Lines on a Sun-Dial

Sunshine nimble,
Loitering shade,
For their symbol
I was made.